I'm Going To WRITE!™

26 LETTERS

lowercase letters

STERLING CHILDREN'S BOOKS
New York

In this book you will learn how to write these letters and numbers.

a b c d e f

g h i j k

l m n o p

q r s t u

v w x y z

1 2 3 4 5

6 7 8 9 10

Writing

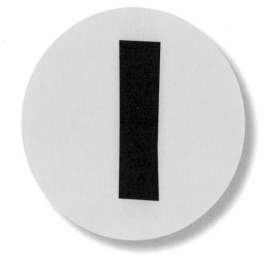

l

lobster

Trace.

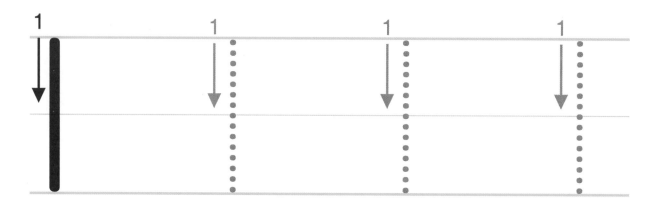

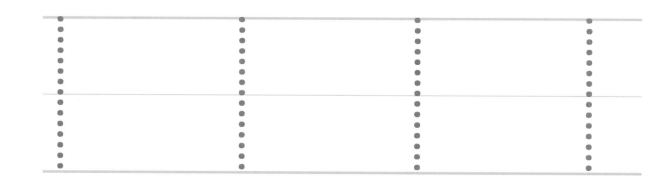

Write on your own.

1

letter

llama

Writing

turtle

Trace.

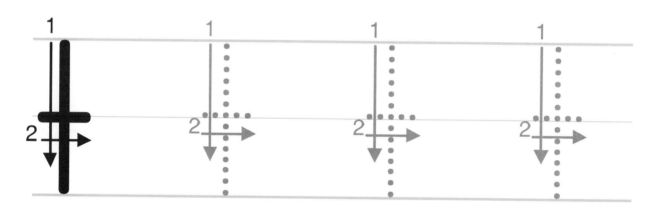

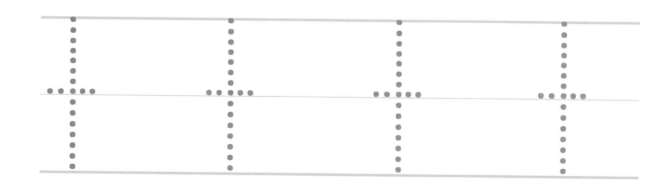

Write on your own.

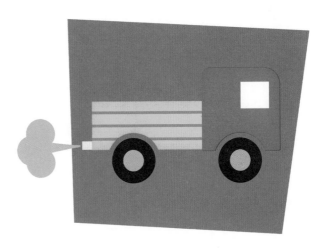

truck

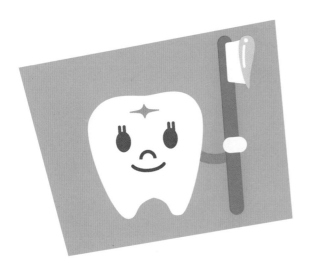

teeth

a b c d e f g h **i** j k l m n o p q r s t u v w x y z

Writing

igloo

Trace.

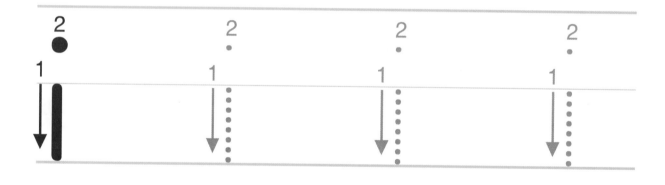

Write on your own.

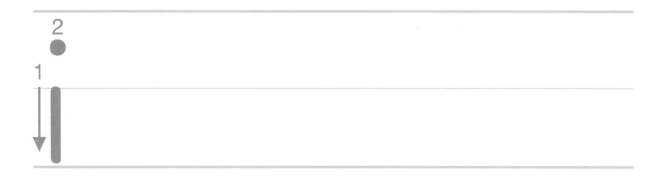

2
1

ice

insect

Writing

jump

Trace.

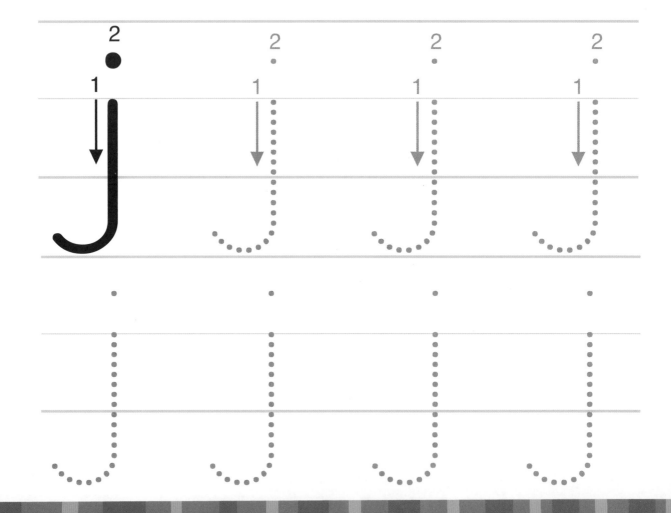

a b c d e f g h i **j** k l m n o p q r s t u v w x y z

Write on your own.

j

jeep

juice

Writing

flower

Trace.

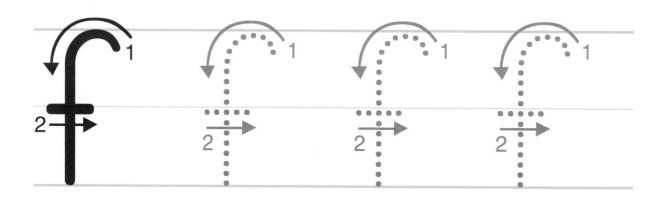

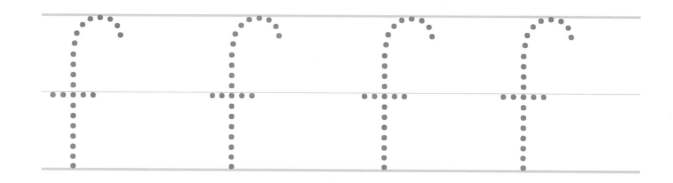

Write on your own.

feet

fly

Writing

vase

Trace.

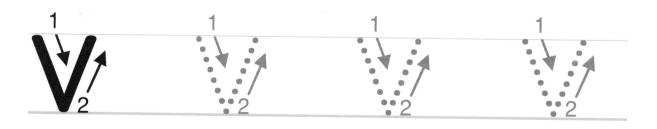

Write on your own.

vine

van

Writing

water

Trace.

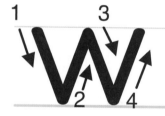
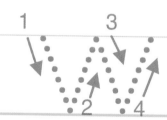
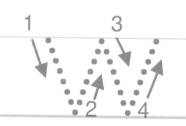

a b c d e f g h i j k l m n o p q r s t u v **w** x y z

Write on your own.

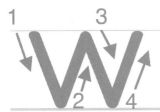

waiter

wash

Writing

ring

Trace.

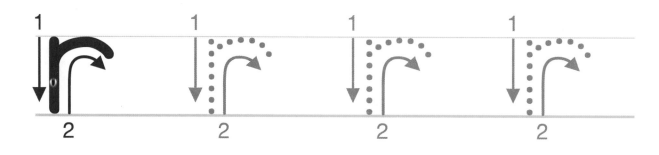

Write on your own.

red

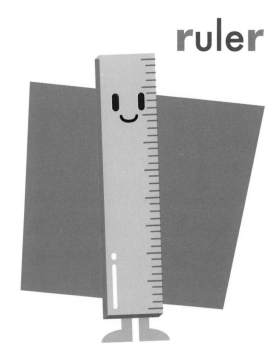

ruler

Writing

nightgown

Trace.

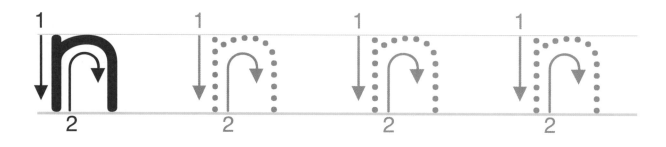

Write on your own.

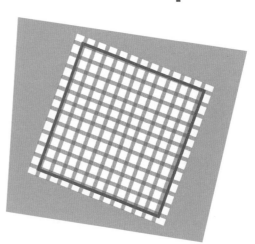

napkin

nine

a
b
c
d
e
f
g
h
i
j
k
l
m
n
o
p
q
r
s
t
u
v
w
x
y
z

Writing

head

Trace.

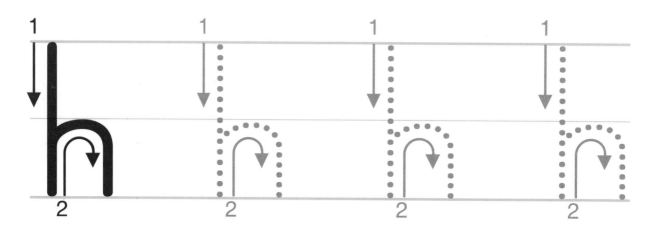

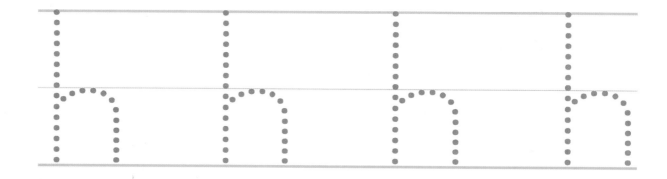

Write on your own.

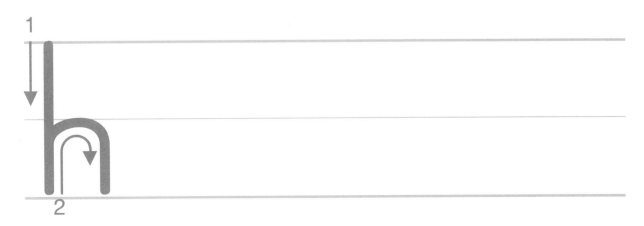

hat

horn

a b c d e f g h i j k l **m** n o p q r s t u v w x y z

Writing

mouse

Trace.

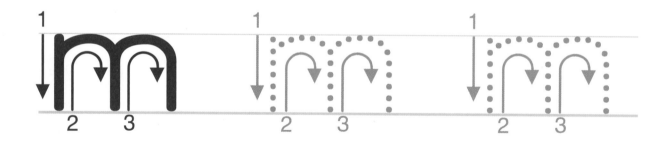

Write on your own.

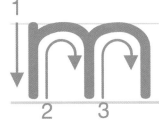

1
2 3

money

monkey

Writing

X-ray

Trace.

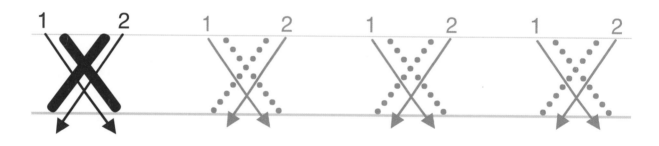

a b c d e f g h i j k l m n o p q r s t u v w **x** y z

Write on your own.

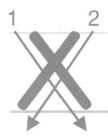
1 2

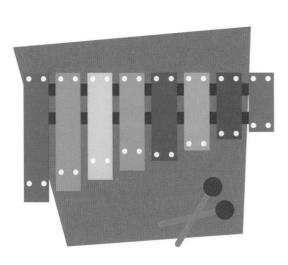
xylophone

o**x**

Writing

yak

Trace.

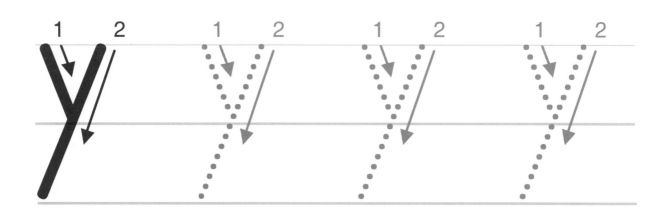

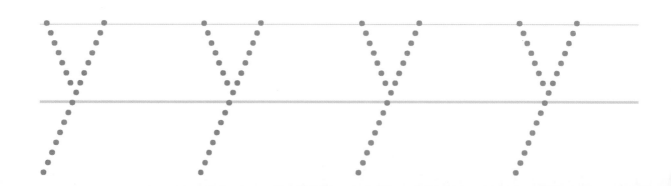

Write on your own.

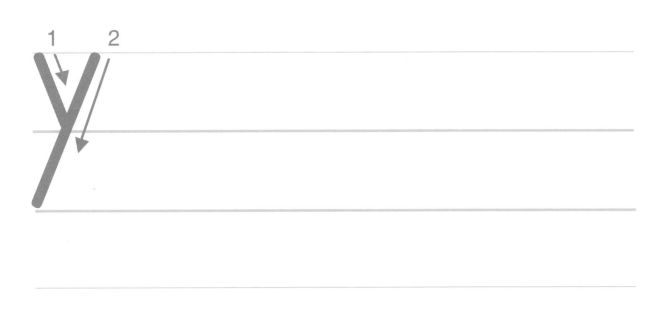

yellow

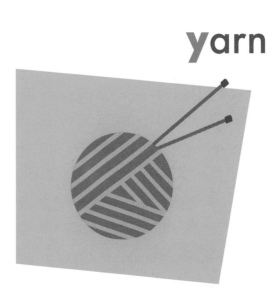

yarn

Writing

Z

zebra

Trace.

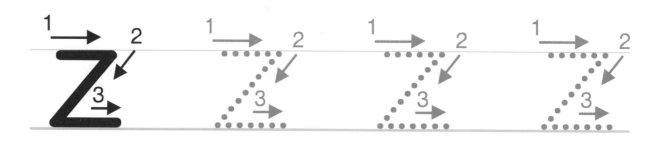

Write on your own.

zigzag

zucchini

Writing

kids

Trace.

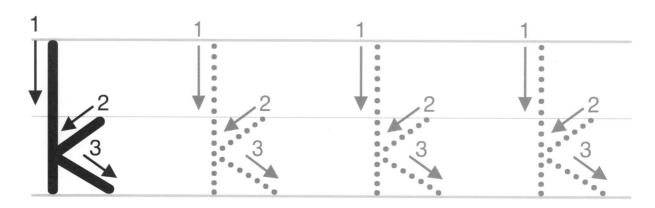

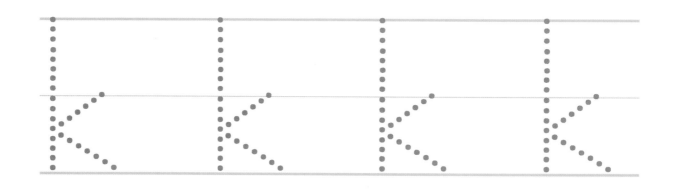

Write on your own.

kite

kitten

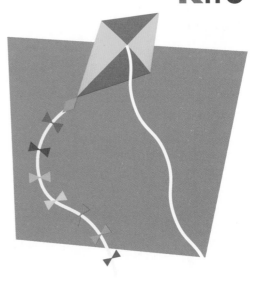

Writing

swim

Trace.

Write on your own.

 S

snake

sun

Writing

cookie

Trace.

Write on your own.

castle

cup

Writing

onion

Trace.

a b c d e f g h i j k l m n o p q r s t u v w x y z

Write on your own.

 1

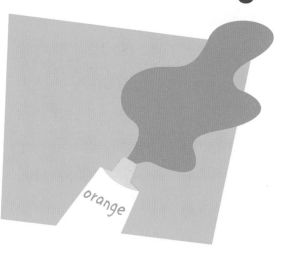

orange

olive

Writing

elephant

Trace.

Write on your own.

egg

ears

Writing

umpire

Trace.

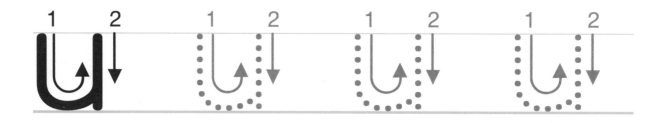

Write on your own.

uniform

up

Writing

ant

Trace.

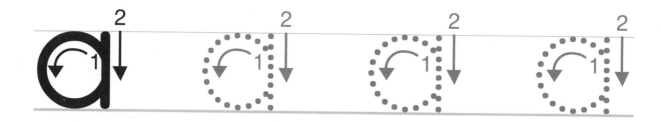

Write on your own.

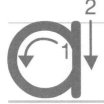

apple

arrow

Writing

quilt

Trace.

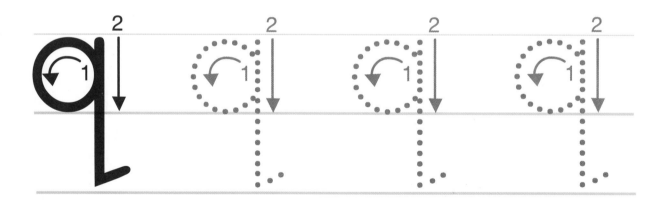

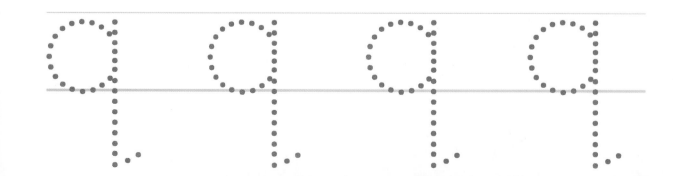

Left margin alphabet: a b c d e f g h i j k l m n o p **q** r s t u v w x y z

Write on your own.

quack

quail

Writing

garden

Trace.

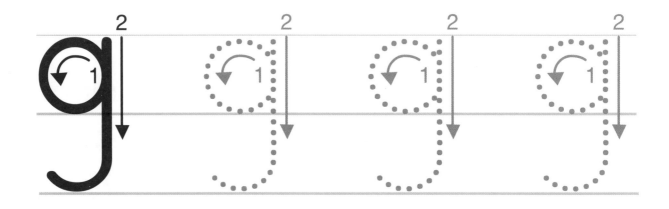

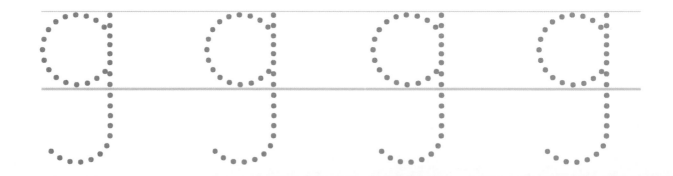

Write on your own.

goose

green

green

Writing

dog

Trace.

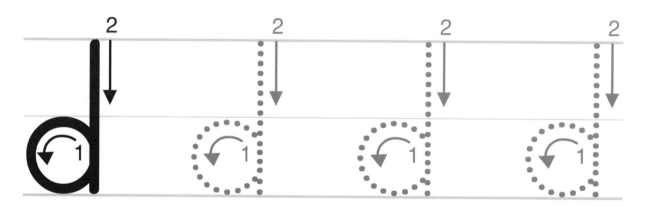

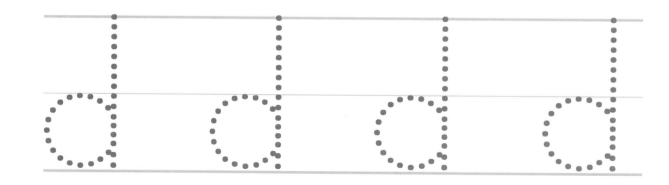

Write on your own.

duck

door

Writing

boat

Trace.

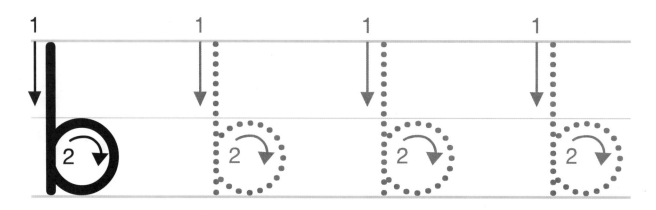

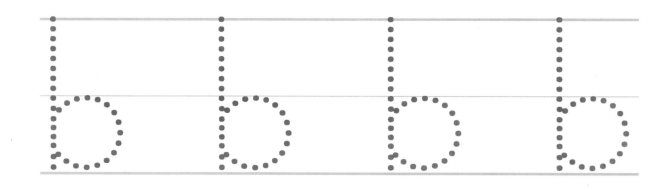

Write on your own.

book

bath

Writing

peanut

Trace.

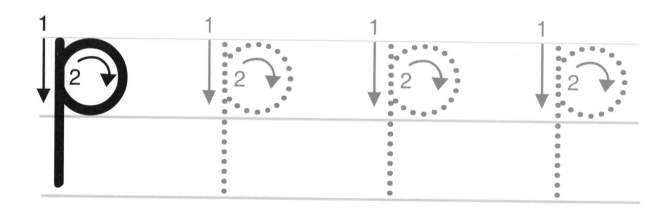

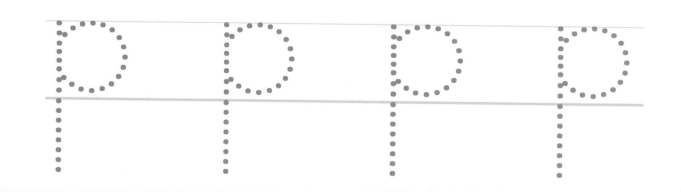

Write on your own.

pocket

purple

purple

Letters

a b c d e f g h i j k l m n o p q r s t u v w x y z

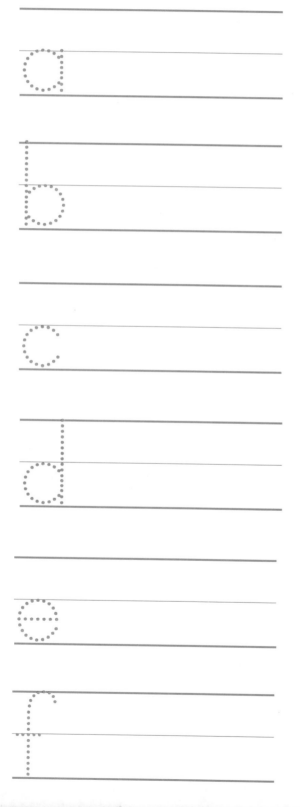
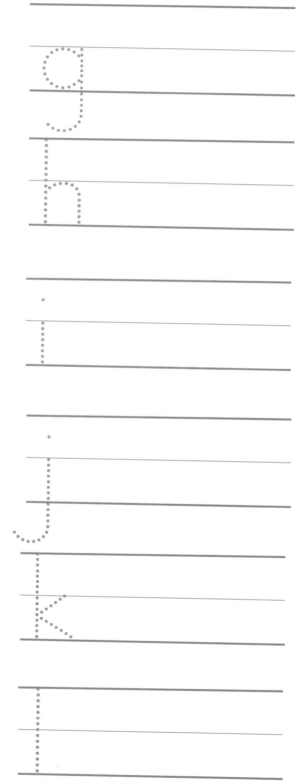

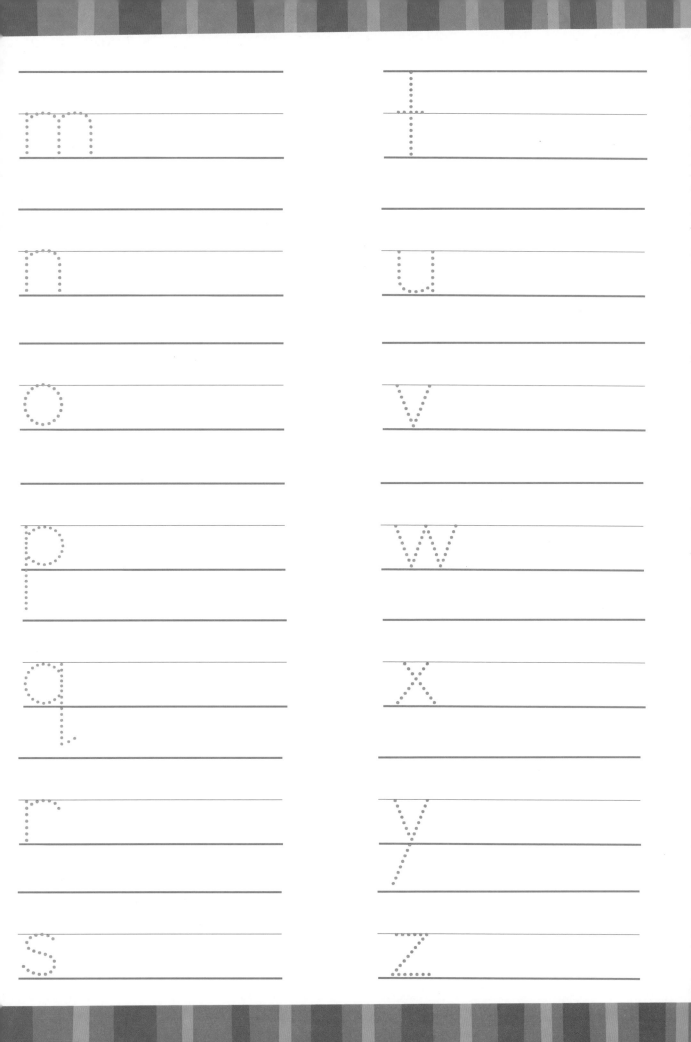

Writing

Trace.

Write on your own.

Trace.

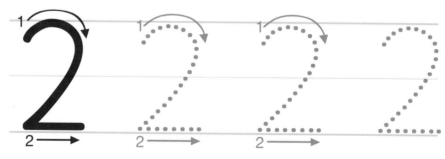

Write on your own.

Trace.

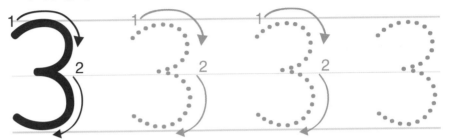

Write on your own.

Trace.

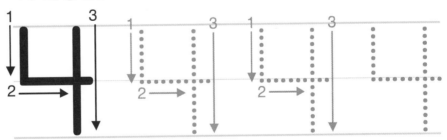

Write on your own.

1
2
3
4
5
6
7
8
9
10

Writing

5

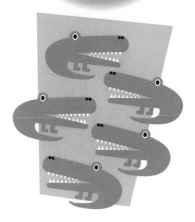

Trace.

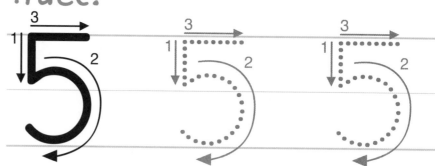

Write on your own.

6

Trace.

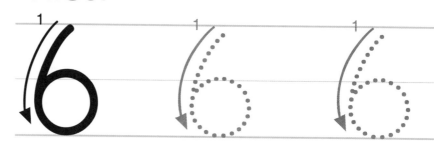

Write on your own.

7

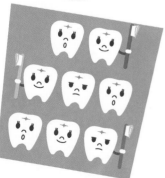

Trace.

7 7 7

Write on your own.

7

Trace.

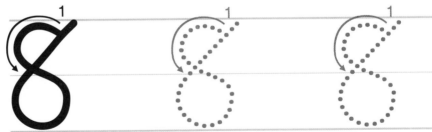

8

8 8 8

Write on your own.

8

Writing

Trace.

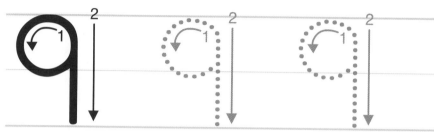

Write on your own.

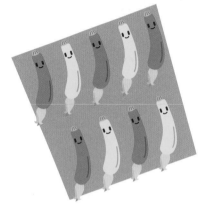

Trace.

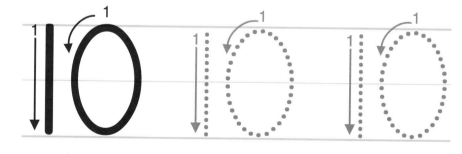

Write on your own.

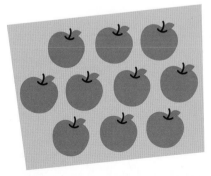

Numbers

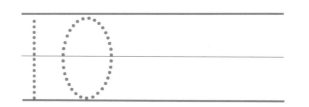

1

2

3

4

5

6

7

8

9

10

GREAT JOB!

_____

_____

_____

date

_____

_____

_____

first name

_____

_____

last name

★ ★ ★ ★ ★ **I Can WRITE** ★ ★ ★ ★ ★
Lowercase Letters and Numbers 1–10